more time for beads

A sequel to the popular book "Time For Beads" with more exciting hand held beading designs.

by Julie Jackson

GPL GEORGESON PUBLISHING LIMITED

All beads used in this book were kindly supplied by BEADTIME, Auckland, New Zealand.

Published by **Georgeson Publishing Limited**
P.O. Box 100-667
North Shore Mail Centre, Auckland,
New Zealand.
Email: GPL@georgeson.co.nz

ISBN No. 0-9582339-0-X

Editor: Prue Georgeson
Photography: Maria Sainsbury
Layout and Illustrations: Andreena Buckton
                               Noodle Design Corp.

Printed in New Zealand

Colour Plates

introduction

Over the years I have developed a keen interest in many forms of creativity using the humble needle. Crewel work and raised embroidery being two other techniques which I enjoy as well as, of course, my deep interest in beads.

Since my first book *Time for Beads* was published my interest in beads and beaded jewellery has continued but developed in new directions. I have also become interested in using beads as an art form. My work has been exhibited and sold throughout New Zealand.

When designing a piece I put together a colour way and 'play', experimenting with various techniques and bead sizes. Sometimes discarding the whole idea and starting again, other times altering the shape, style or form so much that it is hard to believe the starting point! The designs range in difficulty from the very easy and quick to complete to some which are more challenging!

My family have always been extremely supportive, encouraging me to push the boundaries and try new things, for this reason I have taken the liberty of naming these pieces after my daughters and granddaughters.

Thanks for all those who have bought and enjoyed *Time for Beads*. The success of this book has been very satisfying as it has been enjoyed all over the world. As a Needleworker nothing could be more personally rewarding than discovering that others enjoy the same crafts as yourself. I do hope you enjoy reading and using this book also and meet the challenge of the more difficult pieces. Please don't give up! I did one piece twelve times before I was happy with it!

Julie Jackson, September 2002.

How to use this book

This book is my second but has one purpose in mind - to continue sharing my enjoyment of working with beads! This book is a stand alone volume and each of the designs featured has full instructions for its completion. Reference to my earlier book is not required.

The designs are varied. I have also taken pleasure in using some of the new 'hardware' available. The new products create new possibilities which I have enjoyed exploring. This time I include jewellery for personal adornment as well as introducing you to designs which are decorative household items or gifts. These designs show just a little of the diversity of items that can be made using a needle, thread and bead.

This book is designed to lie flat for easy reference. Each design comes with all the instructions necessary for its completion making it an absolute delight to use. It has superbly clear illustrations and lots of them, with easy-to-follow instructions to make sure you find beading as enjoyable as I do.

I have made numerous necklaces with rings - using a variety of different beading techniques from simple beading to netting and peyote stitch. The different pendants slide on and off the rings with ease and can be used to ring the changes with your outfits. It is fun and they look so good. Another new product which is fun to use is 'memory wire' - see the bracelets in green and blue made using this.

Twisted necklaces are shown in different colour ways and using different beads. It is easy to stick to the beads we know and love well but fun to try different beads. Another new and different necklace is the 'tube' necklaces. They have a 'chunkier' look and make a great impact. Simple stitches and striking designs combine to make stunning necklaces.

Pretty designs delight the eye and soothe the soul - see 'Olivia', 'Rose', 'Elizabeth' and 'Grace'. We all like special bags for special occasions - the little silver evening bag is just such a design. The delica beads are dainty and attractive, make the design given or use different colours and your own design to make a bag for a special person in your family.

Vessels, boxes and containers are a new direction. The square box is made with square stitch and is a good place to start when making a container. Peyote stitch has many possibilities and is an enjoyable technique to work - the little round boxes with lids in mauve and cream are made in this technique and are a satisfying challenge for an enthusiastic bead worker. The instructions are very full and detailed and the diagrams clear and easy to understand. these are a joy to make and look so pretty when completed.

It is nice to make something a little different. I have made two pictorial pieces, 'Five Angels' and 'Ruth'. If you would like to recreate a photo of a much loved place in beads - read the simple guidelines given at the start of 'Ruth' and be inspired to make a beaded picture of your own design. We have shown it as a picture but it would look most attractive as a box top. 'Five Angels' is free standing - a different way of using beads, just one more possibility.

Each design is shown in full colour in the central pages of the book where they can serve as a very handy reference when stitching as well as an inspiration. With this book as your guide and reference, beads will be an ongoing delight.

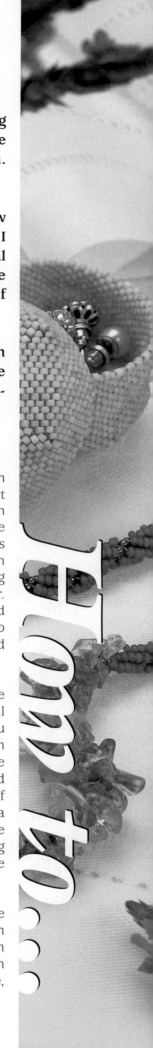

Beads have delighted generations from earliest times. The recent revival of beading means that we are now able to buy from a huge selection of high quality beads. Not only are there a wide variety of beads, there are also new and interesting products available that can be used with them.

In this book I have mainly used Delica Beads and Size 11 seed beads with other beads for accent and interest in the different designs.

Throughout this book we give the quantity of beads required by weight or by the actual number required. As beads are sold in different sized packets check the weight required to work out the number of packet/s you will need to buy for each design.

Needles

Needles for beading need to be fine to fit through the hole in the bead not just once but several times depending on the pattern you are following. As with sewing needles the higher the number the finer the needle. Bead sizes and needle sizes do not correspond. Needles come in several lengths and generally the very fine ones are longer, the shorter needles whilst not so fine are often easier to use.

Thread

Special thread is used for beading, this thread is stronger than ordinary thread and is waxed. The beading thread most commonly available is Nymo® thread. It is made of nylon and comes in a variety of colours. It comes in short lengths on a card in white and black and in bigger quantities on spools in a variety of colours. It is best to match the colour of the thread you use to the general colour of the beads being used. If you cannot match the thread to the beads, use a white thread and then colour it with felt tip pen to match the beads on the stitches which show.

Tiger's Tail

This is a very fine covered wire and is available in clear and black. It is very strong and is used for this reason in my 'tube' necklaces.

Wax

It is extremely important to wax your thread before you start to use it as well as waxing it frequently as you work. Wax your thread by pulling it through a block of beeswax. This is available from most beading and embroidery craft shops. The beeswax strengthens the thread, smoothes down the fibres and helps it to slide through the beads.

Do not re-use thread which has been unpicked ever!

Split rings

A split ring is a continuous double metal ring. Because the ring is double there is no gap for the thread to slip out, this makes it by far the most satisfactory choice for beading. Split rings are used as joining rings. They come in a variety of sizes and are used to attach a tassel to the body of the work.

Ring necklaces

Simple ring necklace are now available in silver and gold. These can be worn alone or as used in this book, as the base for further decoration. By unscrewing the 'ball' at one edge of the ring different pendants can be slipped on and off.

Memory Wire

Memory Wire is reasonably fine wire on to which beads can be threaded. It is coiled into a circle and as the name suggests memory wire stays in the circular shape into which it is coiled. It is available for rings, bracelets or necklaces.

Keeper Beads

A keeper bead is any bead tied on to prevent subsequent beads slipping off the end of the thread. It is tied on loosely so that it can be removed easily later.

Turning Bead

A turning bead is the bead on the end of a fringe. The thread is taken round the outside of the bead before going back through the bead next to it and returning the needle back up the fringe.

Small Pliers

These are extremely useful for breaking a bead that is in the wrong place without requiring you to undo work, squashing crimps, bending tiger's tail and so on. Keep some handy!

Starting and Finishing Threads

Detailed notes on how to start each design are given with the design. To finish your thread at the end of a design take the thread back through half a dozen beads, work a clove hitch or little knot, repeat this two more times, then take the thread back through a few more beads before snipping the thread end off.

Starting and finishing threads in the middle of your work

Bring in a new thread when the old thread is about 20 cm (8") in length. (This leaves sufficient thread to finish properly.) To start the new thread (leave a tail of 20cm), wax then work the new thread through a few beads so that the thread comes out in exactly the same position as the old thread. Now carry on working with the new thread. You will find this method enables you to keep the pattern correct when you change threads. When you have worked a further 10-12 beads finish off both thread ends. Pull both threads firmly to ensure that the bead work is firm, before taking first the old thread and then the new thread down through half a dozen beads and finishing in the manner described above. Try to avoid going through the same beads if possible when finishing off the thread ends.

Reading Patterns

When reading a beading chart the beads are indicated as individual motifs. In most designs one oval represents one bead however square stitch designs are shown with square charts and one square represents one bead. The starting point for each pattern is indicated by an arrow. In some techniques - for example peyote stitch it is usual to work from the bottom of the chart up, in square stitch the reverse is more usual. The instructions given are the way I find it best to work. However any technique is acceptable if you are comfortable with it and achieve a good result!

Alice *Silver ring with green drops*

This design is quickly and simply made and is a great way to highlight special beads. Here it is shown with silver and malachite (selected with a special person in mind) change the malachite to a colour to suit your intended recipient and you will have a gift that can't fail to please!

Materials

- 1 silver neck ring

- 2 grms shiny silver Size 11 seed beads

- 1 grm dull silver Size 11 seed beads

- 12 x 4mm silver beads

- 10 x 4mm corrugated silver beads

- 3grms x 3mm malachite tubes

- 12 x 12mm silver bugle beads

- 7 x 4mm split rings

- 7 x 15mm large silver tubes

- 1 x 10mm feature silver tube

- 7 feature beads (used at the base of each drop)

- Nymo thread

- Wax

- Beading needle

Refer to the colour photograph on page 37

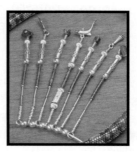

Technique

Threading

Instructions

Cut a 60cm length of thread and wax, use double. Each strand is made separately and threaded as shown on the diagram (see fig 1).

When you have threaded on all the beads take your thread back up the strand to the corrugated silver bead. Do not remove the needle. Thread another needle to the beginning thread and attach it to the split ring securely (I wrap my thread round two or three times) and then take the needle down through the beads to meet the other needle. Tie the ends together securely. Take threads ends up 8-10 beads and finish thread ends (for more information on finishing see page 7).

Make six lengths as above. The seventh is for the centre and has a feature bead included. After the eight shiny beads add a 4mm corrugated silver bead, the feature bead, another 4mm corrugated silver bead, then continue with the six malachite beads. Rather than the silver bead used here in the other six strands, a further corrugated silver bead is used. From this point complete as for the other strands.

Unscrew the 'ball' from the silver neck ring and thread on the strands, placing a silver 4mm bead between each of the strands to ensure they are spaced nicely. This necklace is attractive and so simple. Make a variety of different decorations to hang from the same silver neck ring (see pages 41 and 42.)

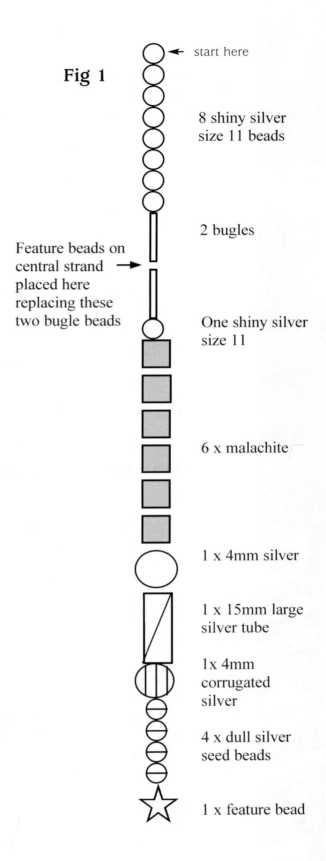

Fig 1

start here

8 shiny silver size 11 beads

2 bugles

Feature beads on central strand placed here replacing these two bugle beads →

One shiny silver size 11

6 x malachite

1 x 4mm silver

1 x 15mm large silver tube

1x 4mm corrugated silver

4 x dull silver seed beads

1 x feature bead

Victoria   *Gold ring necklace with pink netting*

This dainty necklace in soft colours looks lovely on a young girl. A ring is also used in Ella page 42 and Alice page 37. It also looks attractive worn unadorned.

Materials

- 1 gold neck ring
- 26 x 4mm square beads
- 25 x 4mm pearls
- 5 grms size pink 11 beads
- Nymo thread
- Beeswax

Refer to the colour photograph on page 41

Technique

Netting

Instructions

This design is worked down the design area with the square beads at the left hand edge and the pearls at the right. It is not worked *around* the ring.

Cut and wax a 1.5m (5ft) length of thread. Tie on a keeper bead (any bead as this bead will be removed from the necklace on completion of the netting) 20cm (8") from the thread end (see page 7 for more information on keeper beads).

To Begin

Pick up eleven size 11 beads and one square bead and take your needle back through bead #11

Pick up three size 11 beads and take your thread through bead #9.

Pick up three size 11 beads and go through bead #6

Pick up three size 11 beads and go through bead #3

Pick up two size 11 beads (two beads are picked up at the end of the row only this once) and 1 pearl bead and go back through 'x' bead.

*Pick up three size 11 beads and go through centre beads (A, B, C) in previous row.

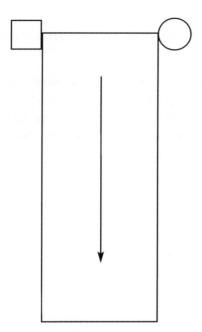

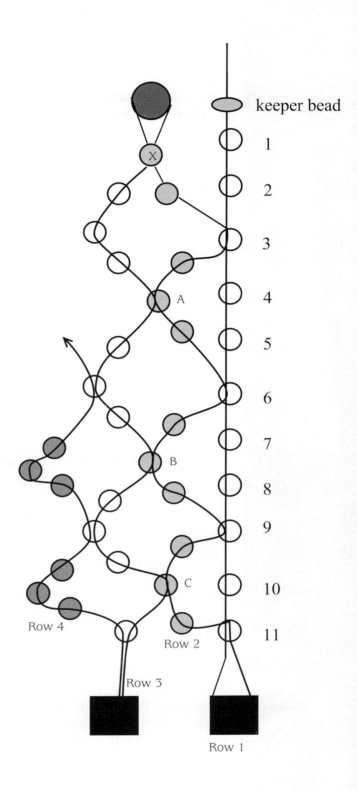

keeper bead

1

2

3

4

5

6

7

8

9

10

11

X

A

B

C

Row 4

Row 2

Row 3

Row 1

At the end of the row pick up one size 11 bead and one square bead/pearl then take the thread *back through the size 11 bead adjacent to the* square bead or pearl ready to pick up three more size 11 beads to continue the new row*. Repeat from *-*.

Work back and forth across the rows until the necklace has 26 square beads on one side (the side to be threaded on the gold ring) and 25 pearls on the other or the length desired. Do not finish off the thread ends as you may find when you thread the necklace on the ring you would prefer to add a few more rows.

Remove keeper bead and the first two beads and finish thread by weaving through the work working clove hitches at intervals along the way. Unscrew ball at end of neck ring and thread on square beads. Replace screw on ball and give it to the lucky recipient.

CLAIRE *Bracelets – Bright blue and green threaded on memory wire*

These bracelets are made using memory wire. Memory wire stays in a circle. It is produced in sizes to make rings, bracelets and necklaces. For a bracelet cut just longer than the wrist measurement so that the ends overlap. For a necklace, cut it just short of the neck measurement so that the ends are nearly meeting.

Materials

- Memory wire
- 10 grms size 11 seed beads colour of your choice
- 10 grms size 8 seed beads colour of your choice
- Nymo thread
- Wax

Refer to the colour photograph on page 44

Technique

Netting

Instructions

These bracelets are made with the size 8 beads up each side and the netting in the centre in the size 11 beads. On completion the memory wire is threaded through the size 8 beads.

Check the size 8 beads you plan to use will go over the memory wire before you start.

Cut and wax a 1.5m (5ft) length of thread. Pick up a bead and tie it on as a keeper bead about 50cm (20") from the end of the thread. A keeper bead

is tied on with a simple half knot *that can be undone later*, to prevent the other beads from slipping off the thread (see general notes page 7). This keeper bead will be removed completely when the bracelet is made.

To Begin

Pick up eleven size 11 seed beads and one size 8 bead and take your needle back through bead #11

Pick up three size 11 beads and take your thread through bead #9.
Pick up three size 11 beads and go through bead #6
Pick up three size 11 beads and go through bead #3
Pick up two size 11 beads (two beads

12

are picked up at the end of the row only once) and 1 size 8 bead and then go back through 'x' bead.

*Pick up three size 11 beads and go through centre beads (A, B, C) in previous row.

At the end of the row pick up one size 11 bead and one size 8 then take the thread back through the size 11 bead adjacent to the size 8 bead ready to pick up three more size 11 beads to continue the new row*.

Work back and forth across the rows repeating from * - * until the bracelet is the length required. Do not finish off the thread ends as you may find when you slip the bracelet onto the memory wire that a few more rows are required

Cut the two pieces of memory wire to the size of the wrist plus 2cm (3/4") with an overlap of a further 2cm at each end.
Turn one end of each piece back 3mm (1/8")and flatten with pliers. Thread the end of the memory wire not bent back through the size 8 beads. Work additional rows if required. Bend ends back and flatten. Take off the Keeper bead and beads #1 and #2. Darn in thread ends. Done!

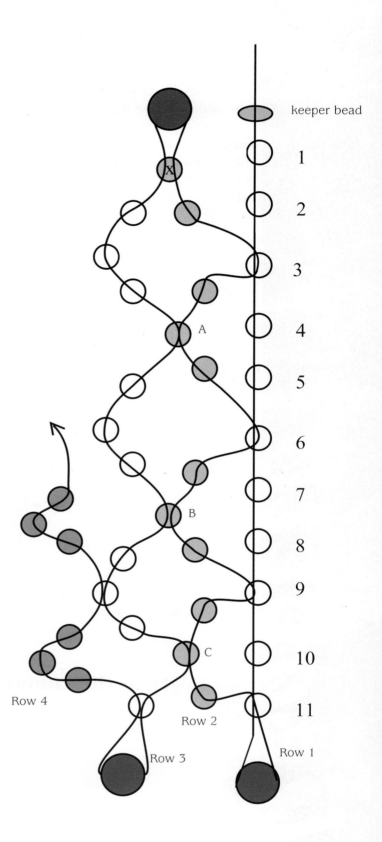

keeper bead

1

2

3

4

5

6

7

8

9

10

11

X

A

B

C

Row 4

Row 2

Row 3

Row 1

Elizabeth   *Bracelet – cream with flowers in shades of pink*

*T*he soft cream background highlights the shades of pink, wine and green used in the flowing, floral design found on this bracelet. Worn by itself it is charming, incorporated into another design it becomes the focus of the new design (see Rose page 41).

Square stitch is a very satisfying stitch for a beading beginner to learn. It has the appearance of a loom worked piece and wonderful patterns can be developed as the beads line up vertically and horizontally. Square stitch is also incredibly strong as the thread is passed so often through the beads.

Materials

- 10 grms Delica Beads (DB) 157 cream
- 2 grms DB 106 pink
- 3 grms DB 275 dark green
- 2 grms DB 163 light green
- 2 grms DB 62 wine
- Magnetic Clasp
- Nymo Thread
- Bees wax

Note: Do not use a magnetic clasp if using a pacemaker.

Refer to the colour photograph on page 41

Technique

Square stitch

Instructions

Row 1

To begin cut and wax a piece of thread 1.5m (5 ft) long. Pick up a cream bead and tie it on as the keeper bead about 50cm (20") from the end of the thread. A keeper bead is tied on with a simple half knot *that can be undone later*, to prevent the other beads from slipping off the thread (see general notes page 7). Following the chart, thread the next 14 beads onto the thread, 1 cream, 1 green, 12 cream. There are 15 beads in total in the row, the keeper bead is the first one.

14

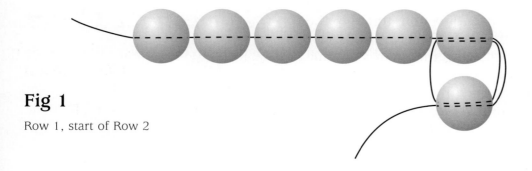

Fig 1

Row 1, start of Row 2

Row 2

Pick up a cream bead and stitch into the bead directly above in a clock wise direction. Then take your needle back through the bead you have just added (fig. 1). Hold the beads firmly between your thumb and forefinger as you stitch so that the first bead in this row sits in the right position. From this point on follow the chart to keep the pattern correct. Pick up each bead and join it as shown (fig. 2). Continue in this manner across the row until you come to the cream keeper bead (the first bead in row one), undo the half knot before stitching into this bead.

When you have completed the second row, pass the needle through the previous row and back again through the beads of the row you have just stitched. This strengthens and stabilises the work. Do this at the end of every second row also referred to as 'stabilising thread'. It makes the beading very firm and strong. If however you prefer the beading to be more fluid this can be omitted.

Fig 2

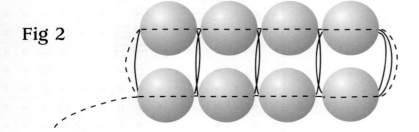

The dotted line shows the path of the stabilizing thread

Row 3

Pick up a cream bead and stitch in an anti-clockwise direction through the bead at the end of the previous row (fig. 3). Following the chart continue in this manner to complete the third row. (You may prefer to turn your work around rather than work in an anti-clockwise direction, work however you find more comfortable).

Following the Chart

One pattern (38 rows). Work three repeats of the pattern (total 114 rows) or adjust size as required.
The arrow shows the starting point
Work down the chart.

Fig 3

start here

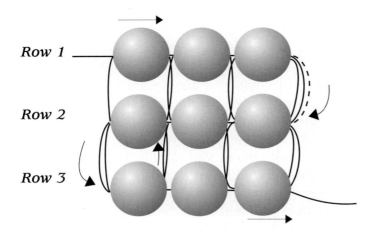

Row 1

Row 2

Row 3

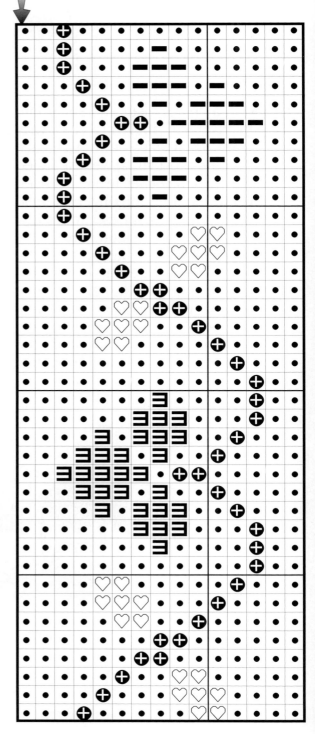

Work three repeats of the pattern (114 rows) or desired length.

Key

•	*cream DB157*
▬	*pink DB106*
♡	*dark green DB275*
⊕	*light green DB163*
☰	*wine DB62*

On completion of the band, still using the same thread, oversew down one long side adding one cream bead every third bead, through the thread at the edge of each row. Using the starting thread oversew down the other long side attaching cream beads in the same way. Attach Magnetic clasp securely.

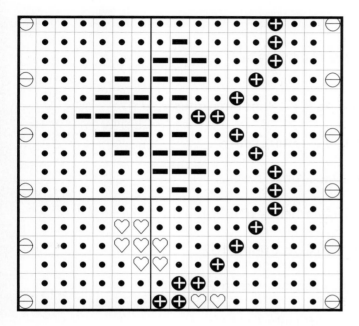

This chart shows the placement of the cream beads down each side of the bracelet.

Rose *Large covered egg*

This egg, with its pearl and crystal embellishments, is rather special. The gentle floral design in the centre comes from 'Elizabeth' and this has been combined with netting and peyote stitch to ensure perfect shaping around the curve of the egg. The central band formed the basis for the colour selection of beads, if you prefer a different colour selection remember a contrast is needed for the pattern to show.

Materials

- Polystyrene Egg 8 x 18cm circumference
- 100 x 3mm Pearls
- 20 x 3mm Crystals
- 12 grms Delica Beads (DB) Pink 106
- 15 grms DB Cream 157
- 3 grms DB Dark Green 275
- 2 grms DB Light Green 163
- 2 grms DB Wine 62
- Nymo Thread
- Wax
- Acrylic paint (pink)

Refer to the colour photograph on page 41

Technique

Peyote Stitch
Netting
Square stitch

Instructions

Make the central band - the bracelet "Elizabeth" following the instructions given on page 14 but following the chart on page 19 (the chart is different). Do not attach the magnetic clasp. The beads attached on each long side of the bracelet form the base for the netting. Wrap the band around the widest part of the egg and join the two ends with square stitch.

Try the band around the egg before painting and if the egg is slightly too large lightly sandpaper before painting it with three coats of acrylic paint. Move the band up and down to find a good fit.

Cut 1.5m (5ft) length of thread and wax. Weave the thread through several beads on the bottom edge of the band and secure the thread, come out through one of the added edge beads working to the left and away from you (towards the base).

Following the Chart

One pattern (36 rows). Work three repeats of the pattern (total 108 rows) or adjust size as required.
The arrow shows the starting point
Work down the chart.

start here

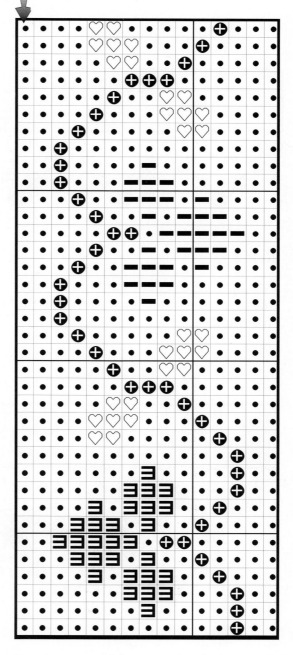

Key

• cream DB157
▬ pink DB106
♡ dark green DB275
⊕ light green DB163
Ξ wine DB62

For placement of the cream beads down each side of the finished bracelet refer to the chart on page 17.

Base of the Egg

Row 1

Pick up two cream delica, one pearl, two cream delica, miss one edge bead and go through the next. Repeat this around the egg (fig 1).

Fig 1

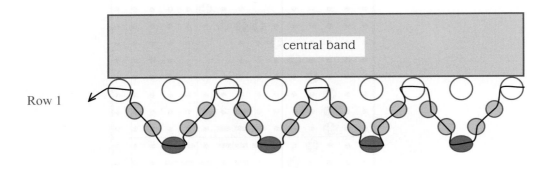

Row 2

Pick up 7 cream delica and go through the pearl, continue to the end of the row (fig 2).

Fig 2

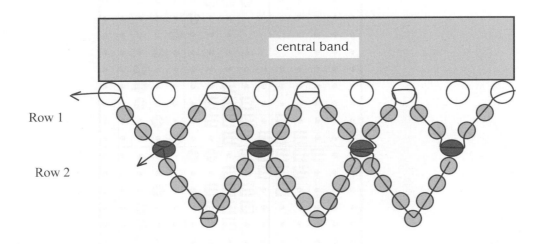

Row 3

Pick up 7 cream delica and go through the fourth bead in the previous row.

Rows 4 - 6

Pick up 7 pink Delica and go through the fourth bead in the previous row.

Rows 7 & 8

Pick up 5 pink Delica and go through the fourth and third beads in the previous rows respectively.

Rows 9 & 10

Pick up 3 pink Delica and go through the third and second beads in the previous rows respectively.

Rows 11-13

The last three rows are worked in peyote stitch. To work peyote stitch pick up a bead, miss a bead and take the needle through the next bead (fig 3). As you are working the peyote stitch, hold the beaded work firmly in place and pull the peyote stitches towards the bottom to stretch the netting. On completion there is an area of about 1cm (1/2") left uncovered at the base.

Top Of The Egg

Repeat Rows 1 to 3

from the Base of the Egg

Rows 4 to 8

Pick up 7 pink delica and go through the fourth bead in the previous row.

Rows 9 & 10

Pick up 5 pink delica and go through the centre bead in the previous row.

Rows 11 & 12

Pick up 3 pink delica and go through the centre bead in the previous row.

Rows 13 and on

From this point on work in peyote stitch. It will be necessary to skip the occasional bead as you draw the work in. Completely cover the egg and finish the thread end off firmly.

Fig 3

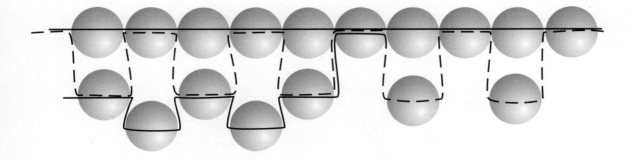

– Rose –

The last Row

The last row is a decorative addition which is worked on top of the existing beading. Bring a new thread in at Row 9 and anchor it securely. (This row is done last.) Pick up one pink delica, one crystal and one pink delica and take the needle through the bead to the left, see fig 4. The crystal will sit in the gap. Continue right round the egg then finish thread end securely.

Fig 4

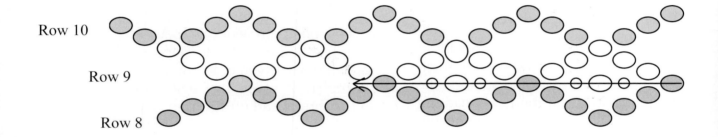

Row 10

Row 9

Row 8

Grace *Silver evening bag*

Bead designs are inspired in many different ways. This tiny bag was inspired by a clasp I had in my "must use one day" box. The pattern on each side is the same, but I worked a subtle shade of pink on the reverse and a deep pink on the front. This bag could be worked in any of a range of colours but a good contrast is needed between the design and the background.

If you are unable to get a frame the exact dimensions of mine, work a sample piece first to ensure a neat fit, adding or deleting beads as required. Any graph pattern may be used in square stitch so now could be the time to use a pattern that you have long admired and kept in your "must use one day" box! Be aware that because the beads are not square a graph pattern will distort.

Materials

- Silver frame 6cm (2 3/8") wide

- 40 grms - silver Delica Bead (DB) 114

- 10 grms - deep pink DB 1338

- 10 grms - soft pink DB 106

- Nymo thread

- Beeswax

Refer to the colour photograph on page 39

Technique

Square Stitch

Instructions

As the beads line up vertically and horizontally in square stitch, designs from cross stitch can be used most successfully in your beading. Square stitch is also a very strong stitching technique so ideal for a little Evening Purse.

Row 1

To begin cut and wax a piece of thread 1.5m (5 ft) long. Pick up a silver bead and tie it on as the keeper bead about 50cm (20") from the end of the thread. A keeper bead is tied on with a simple half knot *that can be undone later,* to prevent the other beads from slipping off the thread (see general notes page 7). Following the chart pick up the remaining 34 beads (silver) in the row. There are 35 beads in total in the row, the keeper bead is the first one.

Fig 1   Row 1, start of Row 2

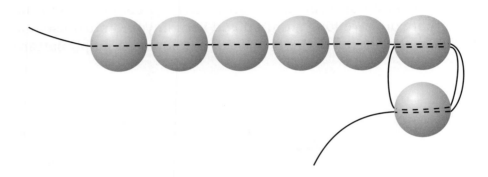

Row 2

Pick up a silver bead and stitch into the bead directly above in a clockwise direction. Then take your needle back through the bead you have just added (fig. 1). Hold the beads firmly between your thumb and forefinger as you stitch so that the first bead in this row sits in the right position. This row is worked entirely in silver beads. Pick up each bead and join it as shown (fig. 2). Continue in this manner across the row until you come to the keeper bead (the first bead in row one), undo the half knot before stitching into this bead.

Fig 2

the dotted line shows the path of the stabilizing thread

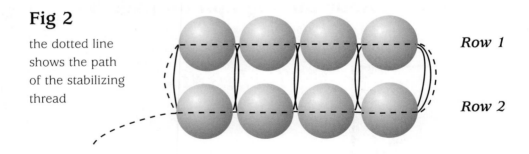

Row 1

Row 2

When you have completed the second row, pass the needle through the previous row and back again through the beads of the row you have just stitched. This strengthens and stabilises the work. Do this at the end of every second row also referred to as 'stabilising thread'. It makes the beading very firm and strong.

Fig 3

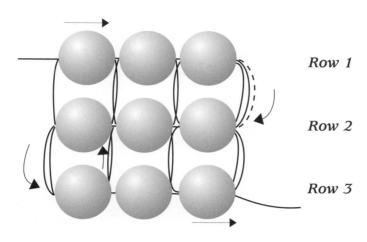

Row 1

Row 2

Row 3

Row 3

This row is worked entirely with the silver beads. Pick up a bead and stitch in an anti-clockwise direction through the bead at the end of the previous row (fig. 3). Continue in this manner to complete the third row. (You may prefer to turn your work around rather than work in an anti-clockwise direction, do whichever you find more comfortable).

Rows 4 - 18

Following the chart work Rows 4-18. The pattern starts on Row 5 and the bag increases in size at Row 19.

Row 19

Increasing on the outside edges

Before increasing on an outside edge, first complete the row to its initial length, including passing the thread through the entire row to stabilise it.

Pick up the number of beads you're increasing by (three see chart) plus the first bead of the next row - four in total. Add the three new beads to extend the row then the first bead of the new row which is stitched in the same way as the first bead in Row 2 (fig 1). Work into all the beads and finish the row.

Fig 4

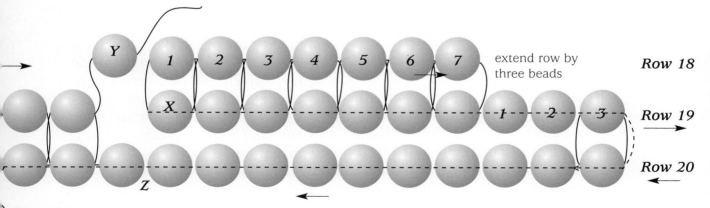

extend row by
three beads

Row 18

Row 19

Row 20

stabilizing thread
X first bead Row 19
Y last bead added in Row 19

At 'Z' pick up four beads, three to complete the row *plus the first bead from the row above* and work back until you meet the end of the previous row bead 'X'.

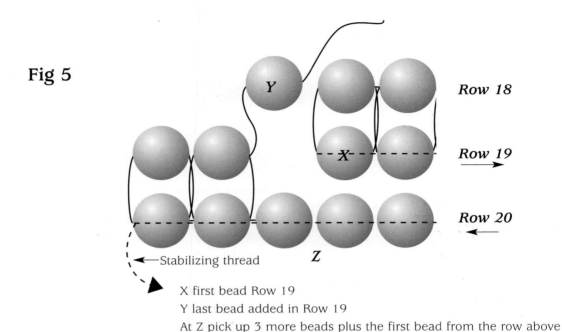

Fig 5

Row 18

Row 19 →

Row 20 ←

←—Stabilizing thread

Z

X first bead Row 19
Y last bead added in Row 19
At Z pick up 3 more beads plus the first bead from the row above

Note You cannot increase just one horizontal row. The increase will affect both the row that has just been finished and the next new row.

With the addition of three beads each end of Row 19 the bag is now its full width. Work the remaining 42 rows following the chart to complete. The Front and Back are both made in the same way.

Making up the purse

The two pieces of the bag are stitched to the frame while they are still separate as it is much easier to handle. Stitch the back to the frame first. Find the centre of the back and using double, waxed thread stitch the centre of the back of the bag to the centre of one side of the frame, go in and out of the holes at the lower edge of the handle working to one side, then work back across the width of the bag to the other side before returning to the centre. Finish the thread ends into the bag to secure. Repeat for the front of the purse.

To join the bottom and sides together take a new waxed thread and join the purse at the base with square stitch holding the pieces flat. You may find it easier to slip your hand inside the loop which will be formed once you have started, while you stitch. Use the same thread to overcast one side stitching through the end threads, repeat for second side. The bag is not lined.

Following the Chart

The arrow indicates where to start the chart. Work from the top of the chart down

Key

⊙ *Background silver DB 114*
■ *Pattern deep pink DB 1338*

start here

Row 1

w 18

19

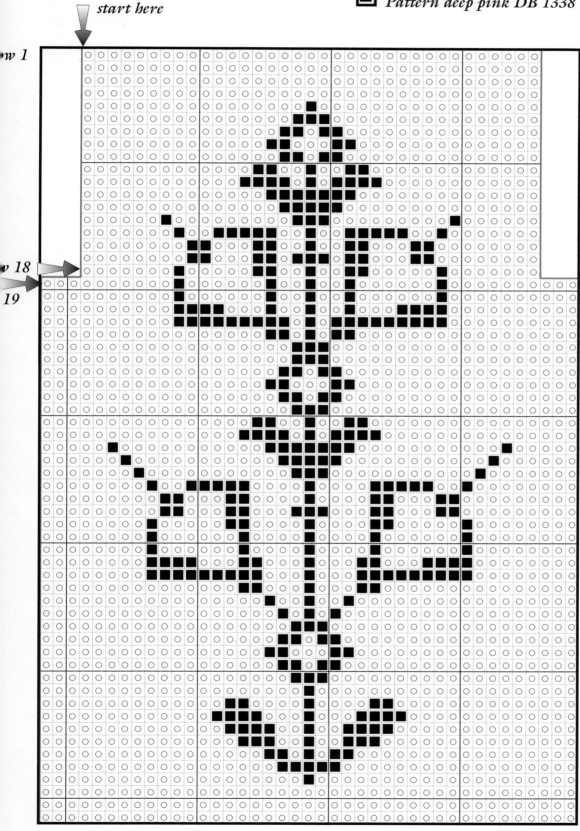

Olivia Golden Egg

I purchased the pretty lemon and amber crystals while on holiday in England and decided that they would be best displayed on a small egg. The same techniques may be used on any sized base, though on a bigger base you might prefer to use bigger beads. The beads are sewn in horizontal rows around the egg first with the vertical rows featuring the crystals worked last.

Materials

- Egg shape, polystyrene 5 x 13cm (2 x 5")

- 20 grms x size 11 gold beads

- 8 x 6mm crystals of each colour: lemon, dark amber, light amber.

- Nymo thread

- Beeswax

refer to colour photograph page 43

Technique

Threading

Instructions

Pierce a hole lengthways through the centre of the egg. Cut a 2m length of thread, wax and use double. Leave a 10cm (4") tail then wrap the thread lengthwise around the egg forming eight evenly spaced rounds. Catch the thread around one of the foundation threads to hold at the base - work a clove hitch. Finish the 'tail' by threading through the beads after a couple of rows.

Horizontal Rows of Beads

Row 1

Starting at the base still using doubled thread *pick up one bead and take the needle under the thread* (repeat from * - * 8 times). There is no need to go around the vertical thread as the beads will support each other. There is no break between rows just continue round after round.

Row 2

Pick up *two beads and take needle under the thread* (repeat from * - * 8 times).

Row 3 onwards

Continue up the egg increasing the number of beads between each thread as necessary but always having the same number of beads between each thread on the same row. (There are 10 beads between each thread at the widest point of this egg.) Finish thread securely.

The Eight Vertical Rows of Beads

These vertical rows of beads will cover the original eight vertical wraps of thread. These rows must be stitched firmly so that the beads lie snugly against the already beaded egg.

Take a new 1.5m (5ft) length of thread, wax well and securely anchor it at the base of the egg by threading it through the beads on the base and making a catch stitch or two.

Pick up 20 gold beads, then one of each coloured crystal, then 30 more gold beads (or number required). Take the needle down through the centre of the egg. Using the same thread, bring the needle back out at the base and pick up 20 gold beads, the three crystals then 30 more gold beads for the second and all subsequent vertical rows of beads (eight in total). Some adjustment may be needed with the number of gold beads you use as all beads are not exactly the same dimensions even when they are the same size. On completion 'fiddle' with the eight vertical rows to ensure they are all equally spaced. This makes a quick and easy present.

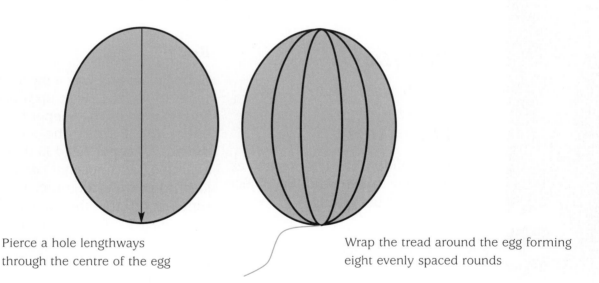

Pierce a hole lengthways
through the centre of the egg

Wrap the tread around the egg forming
eight evenly spaced rounds

Diana *Small dark gold box*

I have always been fascinated by boxes, having embroidered and constructed a number. I enjoy the challenge of the construction. For this box I used square stitch as all the edges needed to be straight which is not possible when using Peyote or Brick stitch.

Materials

- 20grms dark old gold Delica Beads (DB) 59
- 3grms black DB 10
- nymo thread
- beeswax

refer to colour photograph page 43

Technique

Square Stitch

Instructions

This box is made with square stitch as it enables you to construct an object which is dainty but strong.

Box Lid - top

The first four rows are worked using dark old gold beads, the pattern starts on Row 5.

Row 1

To begin cut and wax a piece of thread 1.5m (5 ft) long. Pick up a gold bead and tie it on as the keeper bead about 50cm (20") from the end of the thread. A keeper bead is tied on with a simple half knot *that can be undone later,* to prevent the other beads from slipping off the thread (see general notes page 7). Thread the next 29 gold beads onto the thread (There are 30 beads in total in the row, the keeper bead is the first one).

end of Row 1 start of Row 2   **Fig 1**

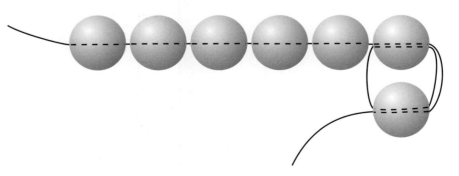

Row 2

Pick up a gold bead and stitch into the bead directly above in a clockwise direction. Then take your needle back through the bead you have just added (fig 1). Hold the beads firmly between your thumb and forefinger as you stitch so that the first bead in this row sits in the right position. Pick up each bead and join it as shown (fig 2). Continue in this manner across the row until you come to the keeper bead (the first bead in row one), undo the half knot before stitching into this bead.

When you have completed the second row, pass the needle through the previous row and back again through the beads of the row you have just stitched. This strengthens and stabilises the work. Do this at the end of every second row also referred to as 'stabilising thread'. It makes the beading very firm and strong. If however you prefer the beading to be more fluid this can be omitted.

Fig 2

the dotted line shows the path of the stabilizing thread

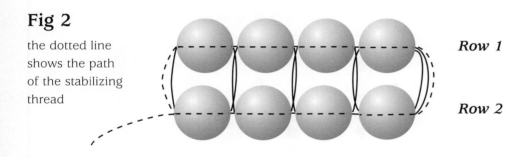

Row 1

Row 2

Row 3

Pick up a bead and stitch in an anti-clockwise direction through the bead at the end of the previous row (fig. 3). Using gold beads throughout continue in this manner to complete the third row.

(You may prefer to turn your work around rather than work in an anti-clockwise direction, do whichever you find more comfortable).

Fig 3

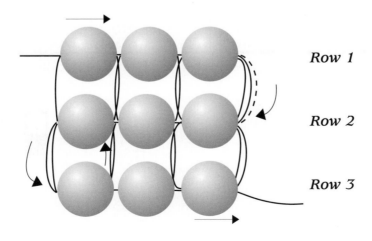

Row 1

Row 2

Row 3

– Diana –

Rows 4 - 30

Continue working in the same way for Rows 4-30 following the chart. The pattern starts in Row 5.

Following the Chart

The arrow shows the starting point Work down the chart.

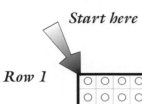

Start here

Row 1

Chart for Box Lid

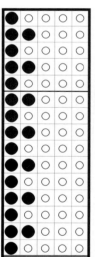

Chart for sides of Lid

Key

○	*dark old gold DB59*
●	*black DB10*

32

The Sides of the Lid

Following the chart pick up one black bead and four gold, work in square stitch following the pattern for 20cm (8") this length is sufficient for all four sides of the lid. When you have beaded the required length attach it to the top of the lid through the stitches at the end of each row. Start joining the lid part way along the side, do not start at a corner. Add any additional rows required to make the sides match the lid and join the end to the beginning with square stitch.

Base of Box

Pick up 28 beads and work in square stitch for 29 rows. There is no pattern on the base of the square.

Side

Pick up 8 beads and work in square stitch for 20cm. Attach to the bottom through the thread at the end of each row. Adjust the length if required and join with square stitch.

Handy Hint
Attach the sides to the base and the lid starting halfway along a side, not at a corner.

Beth *Amethyst Necklace*

Necklaces give a most attractive and personalised finishing touch to whatever you are wearing. This particular design has been made in 'shades of red' and 'misty grays' on page 39 and 'moody mauves' on page 40. The mauve necklace has been made with the addition of semi-precious amethyst chips. These are also available in different sizes and stones. In the gray necklace seed and double delica beads have been used. Many different beads could be used.

The first time you make this I suggest you make it using two different colours or two different sorts of beads - matt and shiney if you make it in the one colour, as then it is very easy to see what you are up to when following the pattern. I give equal quantities of beads so that you can reverse the use of colours should you wish.

Materials

'Shades of Red' Necklace

- 20 grms red beads

- 20 grms maroon beads

- Magnetic clasp

- Nymo thread

- Beeswax

- Beading needle - fine

Amethyst Rope

- 20 grms Amethyst chips

- 15 grms Amethyst matt beads Size 11

- 15 grms Amethyst shiny beads Size 11

'Misty Gray' Necklace

- 20 grms gray Double Delica 107

- 20 grms gray Size 11 beads

refer to the colour photograph on page 40

Technique

Twisted rope

Instructions

Step 1 - Cut and wax a 1.5m (5ft) length of thread. Leave a 30cm (12") length of thread to attach clasp on completion then pick up five shiny red beads and five matt maroon beads. (Wind the end of thread around your little finger to stop the beads slipping off and to give a firm length of thread to work with.) Take your needle back through the five shiny red beads so that the five shiny beads lie parallel to the five matt maroon beads fig 1. (Arrange the beads so that the shiny red beads are on the inside and the matt maroon beads are on the outside)

Step 2 - Pick up one shiny red bead and five matt maroon beads and slide beads to rest on top of the beads already threaded. Now take the needle through four of the first five shiny red beads picked up, plus the newly added shiny red bead see fig 2. Pull firmly into a parallel position keeping the matt maroon beads to the left fig 3. This makes it easier to see the shiny red beads that you are stitching through. Keep thread very firm. A spiral will form as you progress.

Fig 1

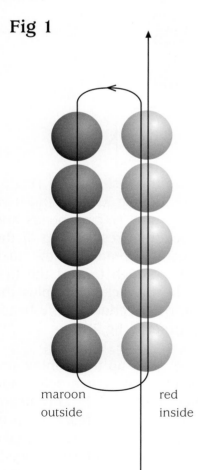

maroon outside   red inside

Fig 2

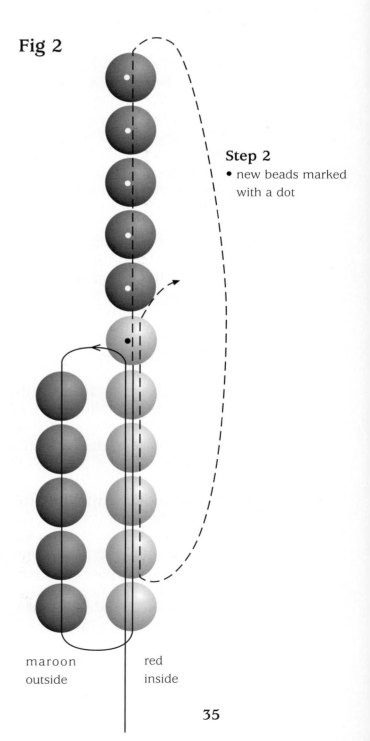

Step 2
- new beads marked with a dot

maroon outside   red inside

To Continue - *From now on pick up one shiny red bead and five matt maroon beads* and slide beads to rest on top of the beads already threaded then take the needle through four shiny red beads already on the thread, plus the newly added shiny red bead* repeat from *-* until the necklace is the desired length.

Attach the magnetic clasp at each end in the usual way to complete.

To add the amethyst chips to the 'moody mauve' necklace

Work for 16cm in the method given above.

The same technique is continued when adding the amethyst chips, but as the chip is a larger bead instead of picking up one shiny and five matt beads pick up 1 shiny bead as before then 1 matt bead, 1 chip, 1 matt bead - still go through four shiny beads already on the thread plus the newly added shiny bead each time.

Work 15cm this way using the amethyst chip beads then change back to the original method and work a further 16 cm. Attach clasps firmly and finish threads ends.

'Misty Gray' Necklace

This necklace is made using shiny beads throughout. If you are unsure of the technique practice following the instructions for the 'Shades of Red' necklace.

To start pick up five shiny size 11 gray beads - these are going to become the inner 'core' then pick up two more shiny size 11 gray beads, one double delica and two more shiny size 11 gray beads. Take you needle back through the first five shiny size 11 gray beads you picked up so that the first five beads lie parallel to the second five beads. Arrange the beads so that the five beads including the double delica lie on the outside.

Fig 3

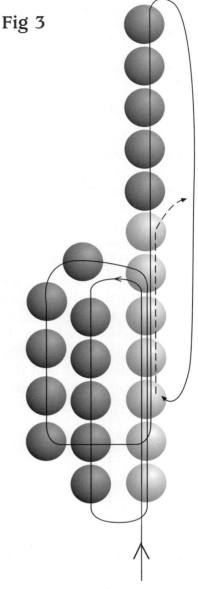

Next pick up three shiny size 11 gray beads, one double delica and two further shiny size 11 gray beads and slide the beads to rest on top of the beads already threaded. Now take your needle through four of the first five shiny beads picked up, plus the first of the newly added shiny beads picked up (refer to fig 2).

To continue *pick up three shiny size 11 gray beads, one double delica and two further shiny size 11 gray beads and slide the beads to rest on top of the beads already threaded then take the needle through four shiny beads already on the thread, plus the first of the newly added shiny beads* repeat from *-* until the necklace is the desired length.

Kathryn

Marie

Alice

37

Pandora

Five angels

Olivia

Beth 'misty gray'

Beth 'shades of red'

Grace

Pandora

Beth 'moody mauves'

40

Rose

Elizabeth

Victoria

41

Drama

Ella

Ella

Pandora

Olivia

Diana

43

Ruth

Claire

44

Ruth

Take a picture from your photo album, a favourite postcard, a treasured memory and interpret it in beads. A box top or picture will give you lasting pleasure every time your glance lingers upon it. Either lay the picture to be reproduced under tracing paper and mark the outlines or for a more detailed chart, lay a cross stitch grid over the picture. Remember a cross stitch pattern can also be used though the pattern will elongate a little.

Materials

- 5grms blue (sky) Delica Beads (DB) 243

- 1 grm grey (clouds) DB 114

- 3 grms mid green (foreground) DB 27

- 4 grms light green (hills to right of picture) DB 163

- 2 grms dark green (hills to left of picture) DB 275

- 1 grm bright green (contrast in foreground) DB 656

- 2 grms brown (tree) DB 7

refer to the colour photograph on page 44

Technique

Square Stitch

Instructions

This entire design is worked in Square stitch. It is a very satisfying stitch for a beading beginner to learn as it has the appearance of a loom worked piece and wonderful patterns can be developed as the beads line up vertically and horizontally. Square stitch is also incredibly strong as the thread is passed so often through the beads.

Row 1

To begin cut and wax a piece of thread 1.5m (5 ft) long. Pick up a blue bead and tie it on as the keeper bead about 50cm (20") from the end of the thread. A keeper bead is tied on with a simple half knot *that can be undone later,* to prevent the other beads from slipping off the thread (see general notes page 7). Pick up the remaining 44 blue beads in the first row. There are 45 beads in total in the row, the keeper bead is the first one.

Fig 1 end of Row 1, start of Row 2

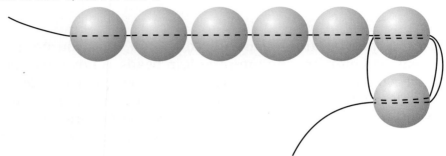

Row 2

Pick up a blue bead and stitch into the bead directly above in a clock wise direction. Then take your needle back through the bead you have just added (fig. 1). Hold the beads firmly between your thumb and forefinger as you stitch so that the first bead in this row sits in the right position. This row is worked using blue beads throughout. Pick up each bead and join it as shown (fig. 2). Continue in this manner across the row until you come to the keeper bead (the first bead in row one), undo the half knot before stitching into this bead.

When you have completed the second row, pass the needle through the previous row and back again through the beads of the row you have just stitched. This strengthens and stabilizes the work. Do this at the end of every second row also referred to as 'stabilizing thread'. It makes the beading very firm and strong. If however you prefer the beading to be more fluid this can be omitted.

Fig 2

the dotted line
shows the
path of the
stabilizing
thread

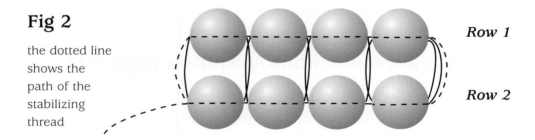

Row 1

Row 2

Fig 3

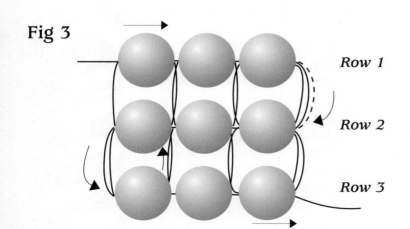

Row 1

Row 2

Row 3

Row 3

Pick up a bead and stitch in an anti-clockwise direction through the bead at the end of the previous row (fig. 3). Following the chart continue in this manner to complete the third row. (You may prefer to turn your work around rather than work in an anti-clockwise direction, do whichever you find more comfortable).

Rows 4 - 30

Continue working in square stitch, following the chart to complete the 30 rows of the pattern.

Mount on silk before framing to highlight the sheen of the beads. Frame or secure in box top as desired.

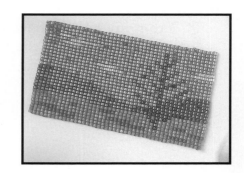

Following the Chart

The arrow indicates where to start the chart. Work from the top of the chart down

Start here

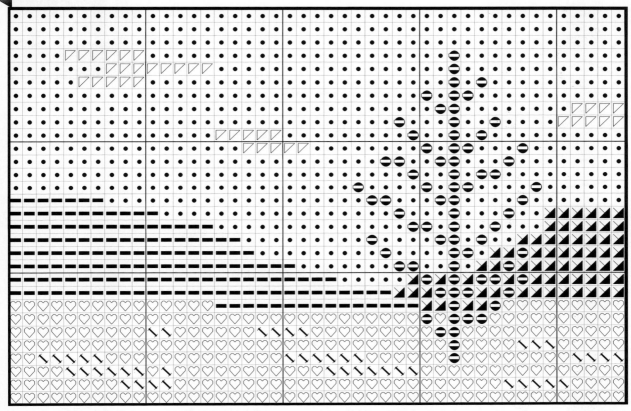

Key

grey (clouds) DB114
dark green (hills to left of picture) DB275
mid green (foreground) DB27
light green (hills to right of picture) DB163
contrast (in foreground) DB656
brown (tree) DB7
blue (sky) DB243

Five Angels

From my home I have a beautiful view of the Waitemata Harbour in Auckland, it was the inspiration for this piece of work.

Materials

- 15grms blue Delica Beads (DB) 113
- 2grms dark blue DB 63
- 2grms gold DB 65
- 2grms antique gold DB 651
- 5grms brown DB 23
- 5grms dark green DB 27
- 5grms medium green DB 656
- 5grms light green DB 163
- 2 grms apricot DB 207
- 2 grms bronze DB 1333
- 5 x 2cm fish
- Nymo thread
- Beeswax
- Beading needle

refer to the colour photograph on page 38

Technique

square stitch

Instructions

The frame is worked using square stitch and is stitched in four separate sections. Working from the top down. Although it could be worked in one big piece it is easier to handle in four pieces. The four pieces are subsequently joined with square stitch.

Top Edge

Row 1

To begin cut and wax a piece of thread 1.5m (5 ft) long. Pick up a blue bead

48

and tie it on as the keeper bead about 50cm (20") from the end of the thread. A keeper bead is tied on with a simple half knot *that can be undone later,* to prevent the other beads from slipping off the thread (see general notes page 7). Following the chart and starting where indicated thread the next 67 beads onto the thread (There are 68 beads in total in the row, the keeper bead is the first one).

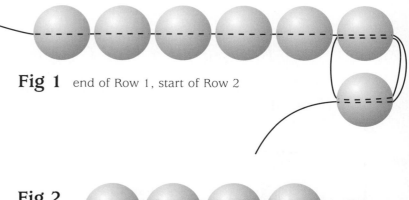

Fig 1   end of Row 1, start of Row 2

Row 2

Pick up a blue bead (all this row is worked using blue beads) and stitch into the bead directly above in a clockwise direction. Then take your needle back through the bead you have just added (fig. 1). Hold the beads firmly between your thumb and forefinger as you stitch so that the first bead in this row sits in the right position. Pick up each bead and join it as shown (fig. 2). Continue in this manner across the row until you come to the keeper bead (the first bead in row one), undo the half knot before stitching into this bead.

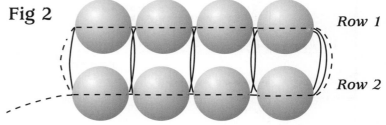

the dotted line shows the path of the stabilizing thread

When you have completed the second row, pass the needle through the previous row and back again through the beads of the row you have just stitched. This strengthens and stabilizes the work. Do this at the end of every second row also referred to as 'stabilizing thread'. It makes the beading very firm and strong. If however you prefer the beading to be more fluid this can be omitted.

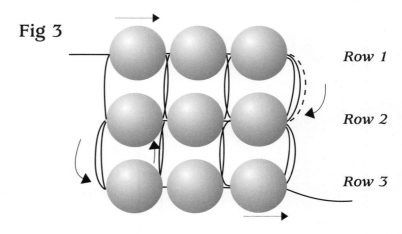

Fig 3

Row 3

Pick up a blue bead (all this row is worked using blue beads also) and stitch in an anti-clockwise direction through the bead at the end of the previous row (fig. 3). Continue in this manner to complete the third row. (You may prefer to turn your work

around rather than work in an anti-clockwise direction, do whichever you find more comfortable).

Rows 4-14

Keeping to the pattern work Rows 4-14 following the chart.

Lower Edge

Cut and wax a 1.5m (5ft) length of thread pick up 68 beads and follow the pattern starting at the line CD. Work the 14 rows in the manner described above and finish the thread end securely.

Following the Chart

The arrow indicates where to start the chart. Work from the top of the chart down

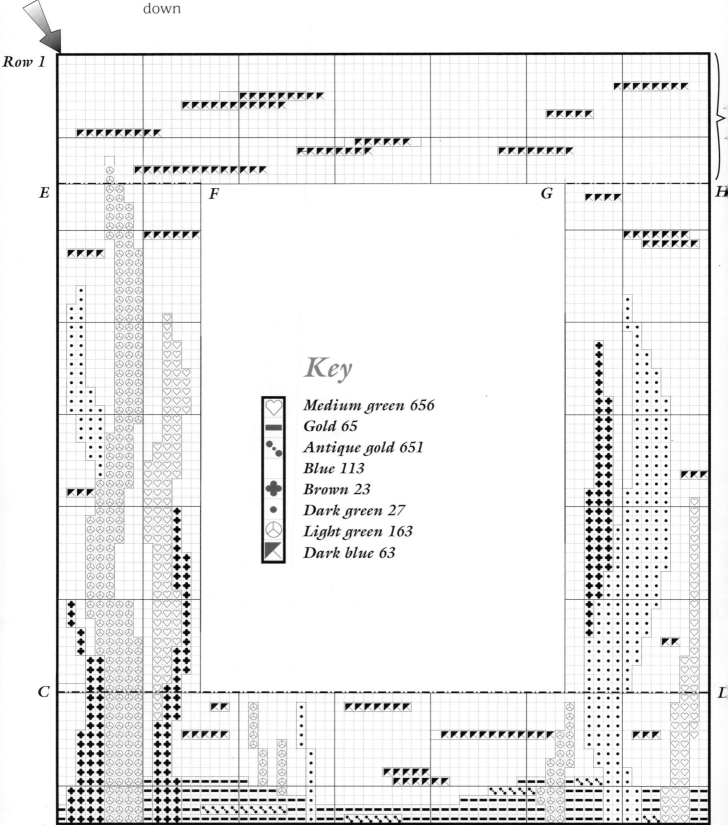

Key

♡	Medium green 656
▬	Gold 65
•ₒ₀	Antique gold 651
	Blue 113
♣	Brown 23
•	Dark green 27
⊕	Light green 163
◤	Dark blue 63

Sides

Work both sides in the same technique as the top and bottom starting at EF and GH. Pick up 15 beads and following the pattern work 55 rows completing each side.

With thread ends left trailing, weave the four separate pieces together using square stitch.

The Seaweed
- seen up the sides of the design

On the left hand side there are three strands of seaweed, in brown, mid and light green, on the right hand side there are just two, in brown and dark green. It is worked in varying lengths, widths and colours.
Pick up 40 beads and return in peyote stitch (fig 4). Work up and down for several rows decreasing the number of beads to make the bottom wider than the top. Stitch the seaweed in place putting some stitches up the full length.

The Coral
- seen at the base of the design

The coral is made from gold, bronze, dark and light green and apricot beads. Make 8-10 selecting the colours as you prefer. Cut a 1.5m (5ft) length of thread and wax. Pick up 16 beads in your selected colour, tying on the first as a keeper bead. Turn on the 16th bead and take your needle back up two beads, this will give you three beads at the bottom, pick up three beads, to create a little 'branch'. Turn on the third bead and go back through the first two beads of the 'branch'. Now go up three beads of the main string and create another branch, do this until you reach the first bead (fig 5). Attach coral securely at the base of the seaweed

Fig 4

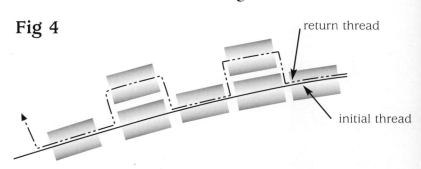

return thread

initial thread

To attach the fish, wax the thread heavily and catch the thread in the back of the work. Tie the fish at different heights.

Insert a little wire rod behind the top edge of the frame you have selected and attach the top edge of the design to the rod.

Place 'Five Angels' on a window sill where the sunlight can shine through it and enjoy the play of sunshine through the beads and your own 'sea of shining waters', the meaning of Waitemata in Maori.

Fig 5

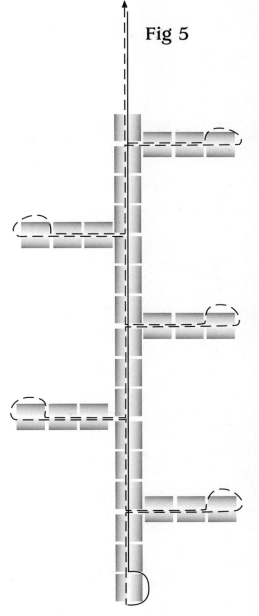

KATHRYN *Multicoloured Vessel*

I wanted to make a beaded vessel using peyote stitch with beads of different sizes, types and finishes all combined in one piece of work. A vessel like this is a great 'vehicle' for displaying interesting and different beads. Any colour-way will work, just collect together a variety of beads in your chosen palette, spread them out and start. Occasionally 'reverse stitching' is required but do not let this deter you from a most enjoyable beading design.

Materials

- Polystyrene ball – 8 cm diameter
- Large selection of beads, various sizes
- Nymo thread
- Beeswax
- Beading needle

refer to the colour photograph on page 37

Technique

Circular Peyote stitch

Instructions

Cut a 3m (3 yd) length of thread and wax thoroughly. Work with the thread doubled and very heavily waxed. Pick up six size 11 beads and tie in a circle. Continuing with the same coloured beads and working from right to left pick up one bead (bead #7) and take the needle back through the next bead in the original circle of six. Repeat with beads 8-12. See fig 2. To complete the row ready to start row 3 take the needle through Beads #1 and #7. Now continue working around the new circle of beads adding one bead between each bead on the previous row.

Fig 1

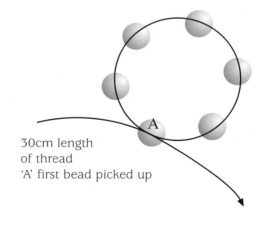

30cm length
of thread
'A' first bead picked up

Fig 2

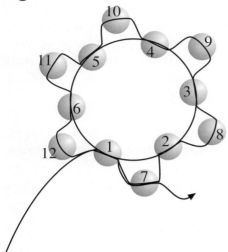

To Increase

As you progress the diameter of the ball will widen and you will need to increase the number of beads in each row. To do this add two beads between each (or some) of the beads in the previous row (fig 3). Continue spiraling out until the base measures 3cm (1 1/4") picking up one or two beads at a time as required, to keep the base flat.

Flatten the base of the polystyrene ball and pin the work onto the base of the polystyrene ball with glass headed pins. These are much easier to remove than small headed pins. From this point on you are working against the polystyrene ball.

Changing Rows

At the completion of each row pass the needle through the first bead of the previous row and the first bead of the working row.

Select three different colours of Size 11 beads and work 15-20 beads in each colour. Continue for 5 - 7 rows in this way. (You will need to add two beads at regular intervals to keep the beading snug on the ball.) When you

Fig 3

increasing

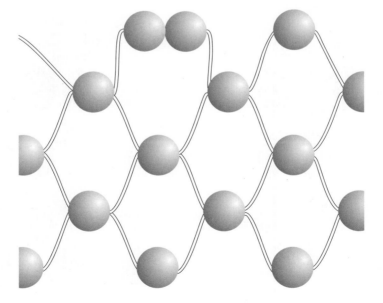

meet a new colour, do a couple of beads in the existing colour before changing to the new colour so they blend - you do not want a harsh line where the beading colour changes.

Continue working in this way using blocks of bead colour, changing colours when desired. Sometimes you may only put in a couple of dozen beads in one row, other times you may wish to do a big block of colour including within it large beads of interest. Work using beads up to size 8 in blocks, anything larger than that would probably be better used as a focus bead.

To add a large focus bead pick up the bead, position it and take your needle through it, you will miss a couple of beads (depending on how large your bead is) then take your thread back into the bead nearest the end of the large bead (fig 4).

In the next row you will need to create a bridge across the large bead. Simply pick up enough beads to cover the length of the large bead before taking your thread back into the bead beyond the large bead (fig 5).

Fig 4

to add a large
focus bead

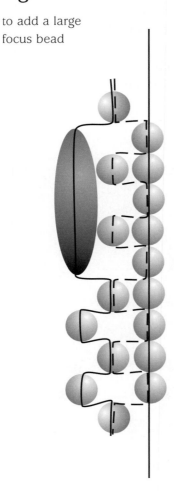

Fig 5

to create a bridge
across the large
bead

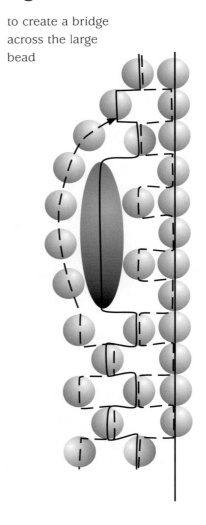

Fig 6   decreasing

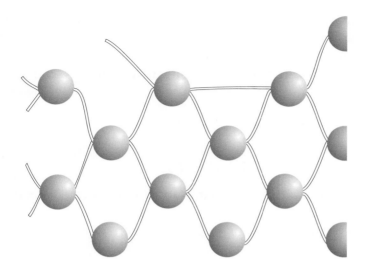

As you work your way up the polystyrene ball move the glass headed pins up to keep the beading in place. Half way up the side of the polystyrene ball you will need to start decreasing. To do this simply skip a bead (fig 6).

Work until the ball is covered except for a 5cm diameter space at the top.

To complete, I worked five rows in forest green seed beads. Finishing with seed beads gives a very nice neat finish. Finish the threads in the usual way, see page 7.

Break the polystyrene ball and remove. The vessel will probably 'settle' a little which rather adds to its charm!

Marie *green and pink tube necklace*

This chunky necklace has impact and style. Made with peyote stitch, it is worked over tube in the usual way, but the tube is not removed on completion of the beading. Casual and relaxed in greens and pinks or smart and bold in black and gold, the choice is yours.

Materials

- Green and Pink

- 50cm plastic tube x 6mm - available from hardware or plastics shops
- 10grms Delica Beads (DB) 275 Green (background)
- 2grms DB 106 Pink
- 4 grms DB 62 Deep Pink
- 5grms DB 44 Teal
- 4grms DB103 Wine
- 5grms DB 501 Gold
- 2 x 1cm beads (to tone)
- 3 x size 6 beads (gold or toning)
- 50cm Tiger Tail - fine plastic coated wire
- 2 x gold crimps - to hold above wire in place
- Nymo thread
- Beeswax
- Clasp

Refer to the colour photograph on page 37

Technique

Peyote Stitch - circular even count

Instructions

This necklace has a series of different patterns which are worked sequentially along the length of the tubing The charts are numbered and are to be worked in the order listed below. The tube ends are then covered and the finishing beads attached. The first and last eight rows are worked in the background colour and each of the different patterns is separated by three rows of background colour.

56

Rows 1 & 2

The first eight rows are worked in the background colour.

To begin cut and wax a 1.5m (5ft) length of thread. Pick up 16 green beads (background colour). Tie the beads in a circle 50cm from the end of the length of thread, (fig 1). Do not pull the beads tightly together – leave space for a further 2-3 beads on the thread. Cut your tube to a length of 43cm (17") or desired length, slide the circle of 16 beads on to the tube.

Note

This circle of 16 beads becomes rows 1 and 2 when you add the third row of beads.

Fig 1

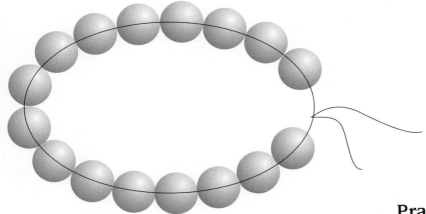

Handy Hint

Practice this technique using bigger beads and working the different rows using different coloured beads. You will then see how it 'works'.

Row 3

To start the third row, working from right to left, take the needle back through the first bead to the left of the knot (bead A). The short tail of thread is now on the right of this bead.

Pick up a bead, miss a bead and go through bead number three (fig. 2).

Fig 2

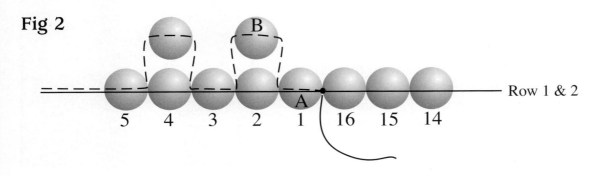

Row 1 & 2

– Marie –

Pull the thread tight so that the bead you are adding pushes the bead beneath it half way down the neighbouring beads (fig. 3).

Continue to pick up a bead, miss a bead then take your needle through the next bead right round until you reach the end of the row.

After picking up the last bead of row three (bead Z) you must take the needle through the first bead of row three (bead A) and then take your needle through bead B (the first bead you picked up in this row (fig. 4). By taking your bead through beads A and B you have made a 'step up' to the next row. At each row change you will be moving diagonally up across the work in the same way.

Fig 3

Fig 4

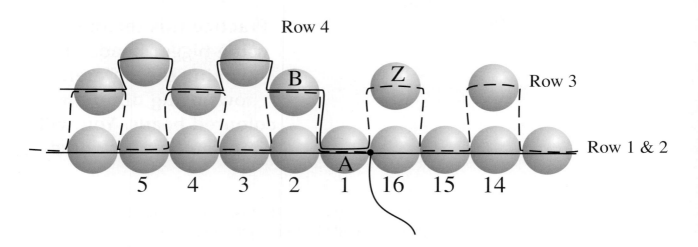

Rows 4-8

You are now ready to begin Row 4. Continue working in the same way using the background colour beads until you have completed eight rows. I personally prefer to work up the tube, if you prefer you may work down the tube, the end result is the same. Just work the way that feels more comfortable for you.

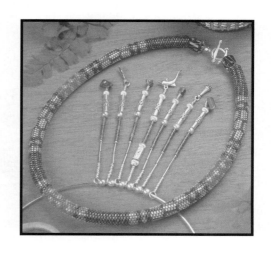

Row 9 Onwards

The pattern starts on Row 9. Continue in peyote stitch following the numbered charts which are worked in the following sequence *with three rows of background colour in between each different chart.* (They are shown in blocks of three for easy visual reference.)

1,2, 3,   4, 3, 2,   5, 2, 3,   4,3, 2,   1, 2, 5,   2,1, 2,
3,4, 3,   2, 5, 2,   3,4, 3,   2, 1

Following the Charts

The arrow indicates where to start each chart. Work up the chart starting at the bottom right hand corner.

Note when following the chart that the same shade of grey represents different colours in the different charts. Always refer to the bead colours given with each chart.

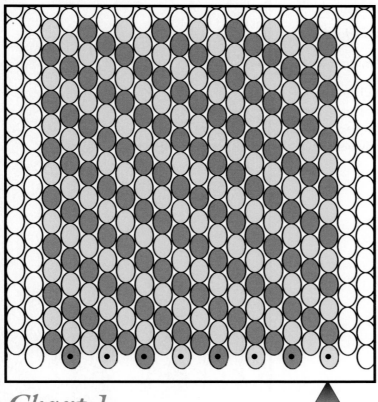

Chart 1

light grey DB 103 wine

Dark grey DB 275 green (background)

Row 1 is marked with a •, complete chart
Work three rows in background colour before starting next chart.

– *Marie* –

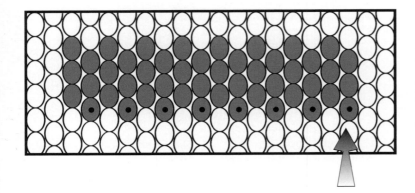

Chart 2

DB 501 gold

Row 1 is marked with a •, complete chart
Work three rows in background colour before starting next chart.

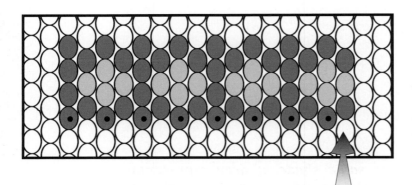

Chart 3

Light grey DB 106 pink

Dark grey DB 275 green (background)

Row 1 is marked with a •, complete chart
Work three rows in background colour before starting next chart.

Chart 4

Light grey DB 44 teal

Dark grey DB275 green (background)

Row 1 is marked with a •
⊙ = background colour, complete chart
Work three rows in background colour before starting next chart.

60

Chart 5

Light grey DB 62 deep pink

Dark grey DB 106 pink

Row 1 is marked with a dot, complete chart
Work three rows in background colour
before starting next chart.

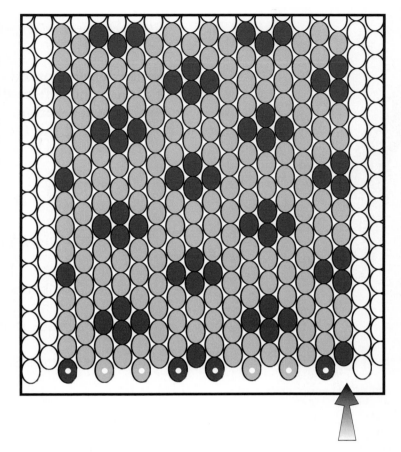

Finishing

Complete the design by working eight rows in the background colour. Trim the tube back to the beads and work three more rows in peyote stitch in the background colour, decreasing as you stitch to cover the hole.

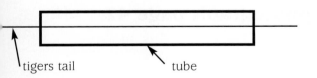

tigers tail   tube

The Tiger's tail goes inside the tube and holds the end beads and clasp. Thread it through the plastic tube leaving approximately 20cm (8") extending each end. On one end thread the tiger's tail with the crimp, 1 x 1cm bead, 3 size 6 beads, and the bar of the clasp and then return the

tigers tail through all the beads and flatten the crimp. Leave a 2cm (3/4") tail and tuck it inside the tube hiding the end very neatly. The tiger's tail is so stiff it 'pokes' in easily.

With the nymo thread end left trailing at the beginning rethread your needle, trim the tube back to the beads and work three more rows in peyote stitch in the background colour, decreasing as you stitch to cover the hole. Finish the tiger's tail as for the first end leaving off the size 6 beads.

Once you have made one of these necklaces I am sure you will be keen to make more - they look so good! Don't hesitate to change the colours used in the design. A bigger tube may be used but when enlarging a design remember that there must be an even number of beads. If you wish to create a heavier effect - use larger beads. Experiment and enjoy yourself.

Drama *tube necklace in black, silver and gold*

T his is another design worked in the same way as Marie. The shiny beads will attract and reflect the light well, which is an advantage with an eveningwear design. The materials and chart are given below. It is to be made using the techniques described in detail in Marie page 56.

Materials

- Green and Pink

- 50cm plastic tube 6mm in diameter
- 15grms Black Delica Beads (DB) 10
- 15grms Silver DB 114
- 5grms Copper DB 501
- 2 x 1cm beads, silver
- 4 x size 6 beads, black
- 2 x silver crimps
- 50cm tiger tail
- Nymo thread,
- Beeswax
- Clasp

Refer to the colour photograph page 42

Technique

Peyote Stitch - circular even count

Instructions

The first eight rows are worked in black then the pattern is repeated twelve times before working a further eight rows in black to complete the design. Next the tube ends are covered and the finishing beads attached as described under Finishing page 61.

Following the Chart

The arrow indicates where to start. Work up the chart starting at the bottom right hand corner. The pattern is repeated twelve times.

Row 1 marked with dots

Key

Dark Grey - Black DB10

Mid grey copper - DB501

Light grey - silver DB114

Ella *Ring necklace with bead drop*

This simple but effective design is shown to advantage on the stylish silver neck ring. It is made in black and silver, and red and silver, but any colour combination with two strong contrasting colours would work equally well. I have used odd count flat peyote stitch which is ideal when there is a symmetrical pattern. The silver neck ring is a most useful addition to your wardrobe as the designs displayed on it can be changed easily see 'Alice' page 37 and "Victoria" page 41 which show how versatile these neck rings are.

Materials

- 5 grms black Delica Beads (DB) 10 or red DB 43 (main colour)

- 3 grms silver DB 114 (contrast)

- 2 x 4mm black (silver) beads (to attach design to silver ring)

- 1 silver neck wire

- Nymo thread

- Beeswax

Refer to the colour photograph on page 42

Technique

Odd count Flat Peyote Stitch

Instructions

As this pattern has a centre point, an odd number of beads is used. There are two different types of edges, or turns, with this technique, one is simple 'Turn A', the other is a little more intricate 'Turn B', both are shown diagrammatically.

The beading is begun at the straight edge near the top of the design - the top shaping is done last. The instructions are give for making the pendant with red as the main colour. The central design is the same for the black pendant but it does not have a silver edging.

Fig 1

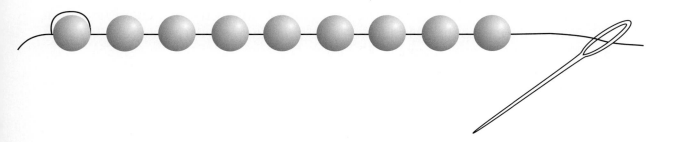

To Begin

Cut and wax one metre (1yd) of thread. String one silver bead on the thread and loop through it again, leaving a 15cm (6") tail. Add 14 red beads, then one silver bead, then 14 more red beads and one final silver bead. Check you have threaded 31 beads (including the first bead with the loop through it). There must be an odd number. The thread 'tail' will be finished off later.

NOTE These 31 beads become Rows 1 & 2 when you add the third row of beads.

Turn work each row so that you are always working from right to left.

Row 3

To start the third row (counting on the diagonal), working from right to left and following the charted colours, pick up bead #32 and stitch through bead #30. This is Turn A, the more straightforward of the two turns (fig 2). Pick up bead #33 and stitch through bead #28; pick up bead #34 and stitch through bead #26, continuing across in the same manner. (The first four beads in row 3 are numbered, 32, 33, 34, and 35 from this point on the beads are marked with a dot see chart page 67.) Keep the tension tight enough to produce the vertical brick pattern but not so tight as to make the work stiff.

Fig 2

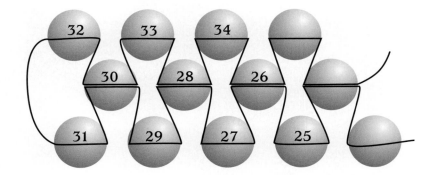

Turn A

Pick up #32 pass through #30, continue in peyote stitch

At the end of the next row a 'Turn B' is executed (fig 3). A figure eight is formed to secure the thread before moving on to the next row. The actual movement through the beads for 'Turn B' is

Pick up #46, pass through #2 #1,

Pick up #47, pass through #2, #3, #46, #2, #1, #47

Pick up #48 and continue in peyote stitch.

In odd count peyote there is a simple turn at one end 'turn A' alternating with a more complicated turn at the other end 'turn B'.

Stitch following the chart until it is time to begin decreasing.

Fig 3

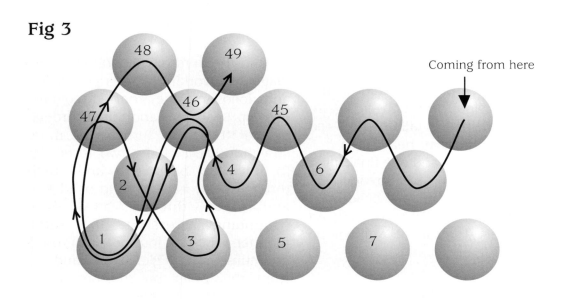

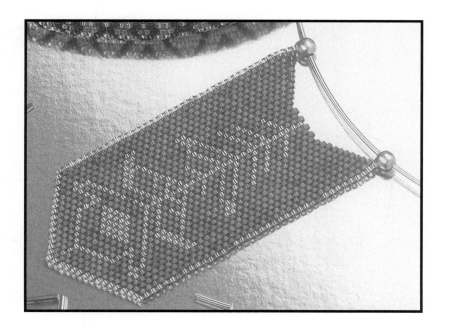

Following The Chart

The chart given is for the red and silver necklace. The Red design is edged in silver, the Black is not. The design is worked from the top down this means that you work from the bottom of the chart up. The arrow shows the starting point

Key

light grey - red
dark grey - silver

X = overlap to next chart

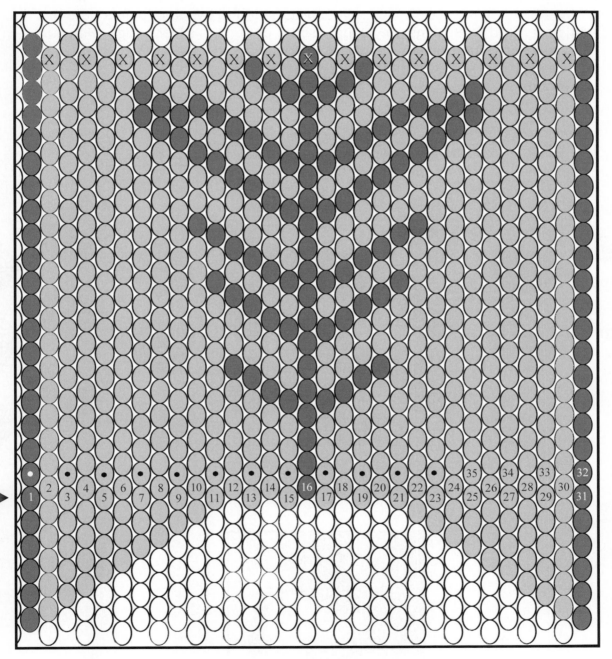

The first 31 beads picked up become Rows 1&2.

The first four beads in Row 3 are numbered 32 + 35 from
  this point on the beads are marked with a dot.

The top is done last.

Decreasing

This design comes down to a point of one single bead. The decreasing is accomplished by omitting beads at the end of each row.

Follow the path of the thread in fig 4

Pick up #47 (last bead in the row). Pass through #37, #25, #36, #24, #25, #37, #47,
Add next bead #48, continue along the row in the usual manner decreasing in the same way at the end of every row.

As some of the beads will have many threads going through them, you may find it easier to switch to a smaller needle. Finish thread.

Join a new thread to complete the two small triangles at the top of the design. Bead following the chart decreasing as required. Sew a 4mm bead on the two top points (these slide onto the silver ring). Finish thread.

Fig 4   Decreasing - numbers do not relate to actual design

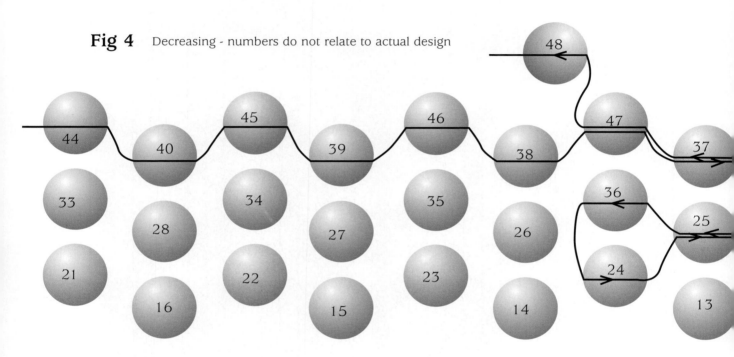

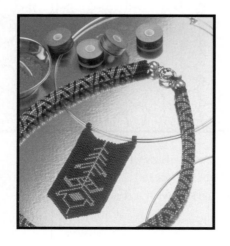

X = overlap from previous chart

Pandora

I always enjoy a challenge and found creating these little beaded containers most challenging and satisfying. I chose to work in peyote stitch as I like the attractive pattern that is formed as you increase bead numbers. The sides could have a stripe running round or a row of simple flowers. I chose to keep the containers themselves quite plain but had fun decorating the lids. I put a covered silk card in the base and the lid which has made them quite sturdy. The instructions are given here for the mauve box - the cream box is made in the same way, it is just bigger.

Materials

- Mauve box 25 grms Delica Beads (DB) 354 (Cream box 30grms DB 353)

- Beads for embellishment

- Nymo thread

- Wax

- Beading needle

Refer to the colour photograph on page 42

Technique

Circular Peyote
Tubular Peyote

Instructions

These containers are made using circular peyote stitch for the base and lid and tubular even count peyote for the sides of the base and lid. The base and lid are made first and then the sides are made separately and attached.

Base and lid

The lid is made in exactly the same way as the base except that an additional three rows are worked to make the lid slightly larger than the base so that it fits over it when completed. At the end of the instructions for the base the instructions for the additional rows required to make the lid are given. A diagram is given of the stitching of the base (lid) showing the addition of the beads and the path of the needle. Refer to it as you stitch for additional assistance.

Row 1

Cut a 1.5m (5ft) length of thread and wax well. Pick up six beads and tie in a circle. Working from right to left pass the needle back through the first bead 'A'.

Row 2

Pick up one bead (bead #7) and take the needle back through the next bead in the original circle of six. Repeat with beads 8-12. See fig 2.

To complete the row ready to start row 3 take the needle through Beads #1 and #7.

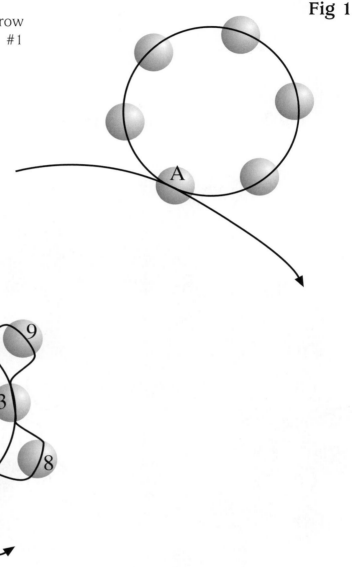

Fig 1

Fig 2

Changing Rows

At the completion of each row pass the needle through the *first* bead of the previous row and the *first* bead of the working row.

I have given detailed instructions for beading this container - however when you are making it yourself you may find you need to adjust the number of beads added - as individual tension varies and beads also vary in size.

Row 3

Pick up two beads and take the needle through each bead in the previous row. This gives you beads #13-24.
To change the row take the needle through Beads #7 and #13.

Row 4

Pick up one bead and take the needle through each bead for the entire row. (Beads 25-36)
To change the row take the needle through Beads #13 and #25.

Fig 3   note alternate rows of beads are shaded

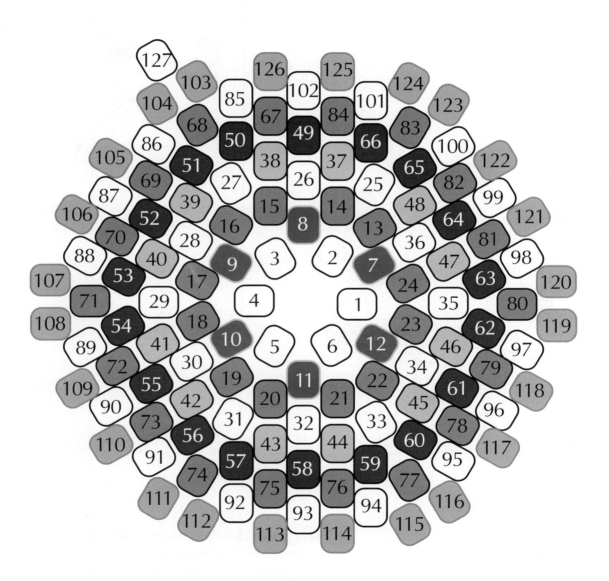

Row 5

Pick up one bead and take the needle through each bead for the entire row. (Beads 37-48)
To change the row take the needle through Beads #25 and #37.

Row 6

In this row one and two beads are picked up alternately.
Pick up one bead and take the needle through the next bead, then pick up two beads and take the needle through the next bead for the entire row. Repeat from *-* to complete the round. (Beads 49-66)
To change the row take the needle through Beads # 37 and #49.

Row 7

Pick up one bead and take the needle through each bead for the entire row. (Beads 67-84)
To change the row take the needle through Beads #49 and #67.

Row 8

Pick up one bead and take the needle through the next bead for the entire row. (Beads 85-102)
To change the row take the needle through Beads #67 and #85.

Row 9

Pick up two beads and go through the next bead. Pick up one bead twice. Repeat from *-* to complete the round. (Beads 103-126)
To change the row take the needle through Beads #85 and #103.

Rows 10 and 11

Not shown in diagramatic form from this point.
Pick up one bead and take the needle through each bead for the entire row.

Row 12

Pick up one bead and take the needle through the next bead three times, then pick up two beads and go through the next bead. Repeat from *-*

Rows 13 and 14

Pick up one bead and take the needle through each bead for the entire row.

Row 15

Pick up one bead and take the needle through the next bead two times, then pick up two beads and take the needle through the next bead.
Pick up one bead and take the needle through the next bead four times, then pick up two beads and take the needle through the next bead. Repeat from *-* to complete the round.

Rows 16 and 17

Pick up one bead and take the needle through the next bead.

Row 18

Pick up one bead and take the needle through the next bead. *Pick up two beads and take the needle through the next bead, Pick up *one* bead and take the needle through the next bead *five* times.* Repeat from *-* to complete the round.

Rows 19 and 20

Pick up one bead and take the needle through the next bead for the entire row.

Row 21

Pick up *two* beads and take the needle through the next bead then pick up *one* bead and take the needle through the next bead six times.

Row 22

Final row of Base Pick up one bead and take the needle through the next bead for the entire row. There are 48 beads in the final row of the base.

These 22 rows complete the base of the mauve container, which is 4 cm in diameter. The cream container is 5.5 cm in diameter. To make the larger container, continue in the same manner adjusting the number of beads added each row to ensure that a nice 'flat' base is obtained.

The lid has to be slightly larger than the base so that it will fit nicely over the base when completed. For both the mauve and cream containers work an extra three rows when making the lid.

Extra three rows for lid of mauve container

Row 23

Pick up one bead and take the needle through the next bead for the entire row.

Row 24

Pick up one bead and take the needle through the next bead seven times, pick up two beads and take the needle through the next bead once. Repeat from *-* to complete the row.

Row 25

Pick up one bead and take the needle through the next bead for the entire row. There are 54 beads in the final row of the lid

Mauve Container

To make the side of the base and the lid

The sides of the base and lid are made in even count tubular peyote stitch.
In each case the number of beads required to make the sides is double that of the final row of the circumference of the base (and lid). On the base 96 is double the 48 beads in the last row of the base and the lid has 108 beads, double the 54 in the final row of the circumference. This is because when the sides are joined to the base (and lid) one bead is picked up from the top and one from the side and it fits together like a zip.

The side of the lid is made in the same way as the side of the base of the container except that it is slightly larger in circumference and shallower in depth. *The instructions for the lid are given in brackets after the instructions for the side of the base.*

Fig 4

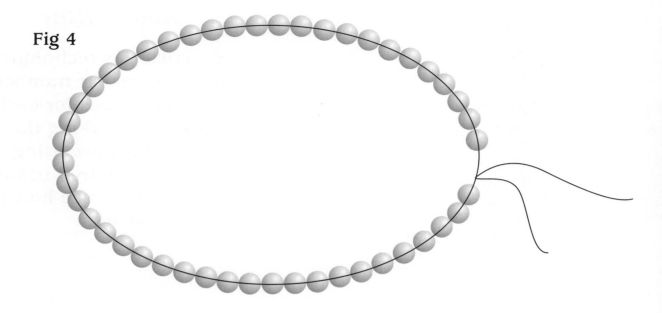

Cut and wax a 1.5m (5ft) length of thread. Tie 96 beads* (108 beads) in a circle 50 cm from the end of the length of thread, (fig. 4). Do not pull the beads tightly together – leave space for a further 2-3 beads on the thread. Cut your tube lengthwise, slide the circle of 96 (108) beads on to the tube squashing the tube in so that the beads rest on it firmly but are not stretched tightly. Tape the tube to the correct size.

Note This circle of 96 (108) beads becomes rows 1 & 2 when you add the third row of beads.

Row 3

To start the third row, working from right to left, take the needle back through the first bead to the left of the knot (bead A). The short tail of thread is now on the right of this bead.

Pick up a bead, miss a bead and go through bead number three (fig. 5). Pull the thread up tight so that the bead you are adding pushes the bead beneath it half way down the neighbouring beads (fig. 6).

Fig 5

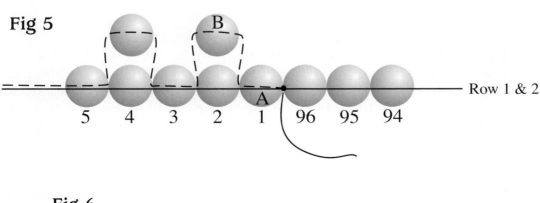

Fig 6

Continue to pick up a bead, miss a bead then take your needle through the next bead right round until you reach the end of the row.

After picking up the last bead of row three (bead Z) you must take the needle through the first bead of row three (bead A) and then take your needle through bead B (the first bead you picked up in this row) (fig. 7). By taking your bead through beads A and B you have made a 'step up' to the next row. At each row change you will be moving diagonally up across the work in the same way.

Handy Hint

Practice this technique using a smaller number of bigger beads for each row and working the different rows using different coloured beads. You will then see how it 'works'.

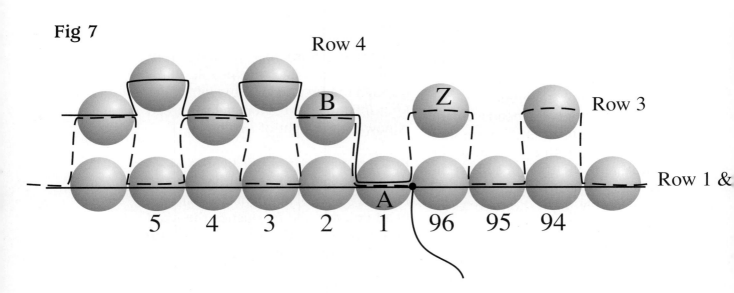

Fig 7

Row 4

B   Z   Row 3

A   Row 1 &

5   4   3   2   1   96   95   94

I personally prefer to work up the tube if you prefer you may work down the tube, the end result is the same. Just work the way that feels more comfortable for you.

Row 4 - 22 (4-14)

Continue working remembering that after picking up the last bead of the row you must take the needle through the first bead of the row and then through the first bead you picked up in this row, then pick up a new bead and continue the new row. (Refer to fig. 7 for the steps involved).

When you have completed 22 (14) rows. Finish off the thread, for detailed information on starting and finishing threads refer to page 7.

To attach the side of the base to the base

To attach the sides to the base or the lid cut and wax a 1m (3ft) length of thread and secure in the base (lid) coming out through an 'up' bead - that is a bead that is standing up.

Taking the needle through the beads from right to left. Pick up one 'up' bead from the side and the base alternately. The beads will close like a zip. Pull the thread firmly and finish the thread end in the usual way. The finished appearance will be hexagonal.

To decorate the lid

Cut a 50cm (20") length of thread and wax. Attach firmly inside the centre of the lid. Select beads - bugle, seed, leaves etc. Pick up a small strand of decorative beads and return to the back. Catch the stitch and return to the front, add more beads in the same way.

Finishing

Cut a piece of card to fit in the base (and lid) cover it with a little batting and then silk or your chosen fabric. Stitch in place from the outside by going through a bead then catching the fabric. The bottom will be concave. It is the nature of the bead, as it is not square a wide edge is against a narrow edge.

– Chart–

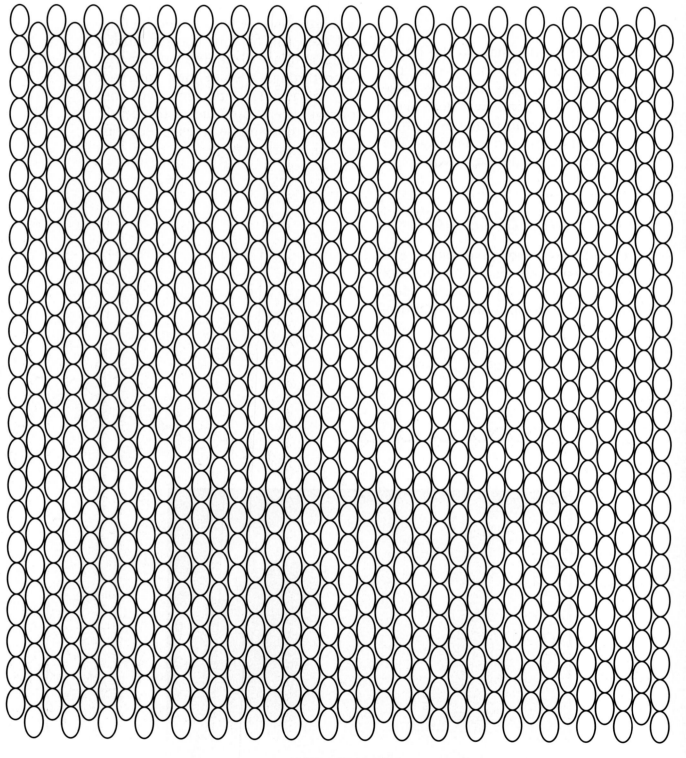

Use chart this way for Circular Brick Stitch

Use chart this way for Peyote Stitch

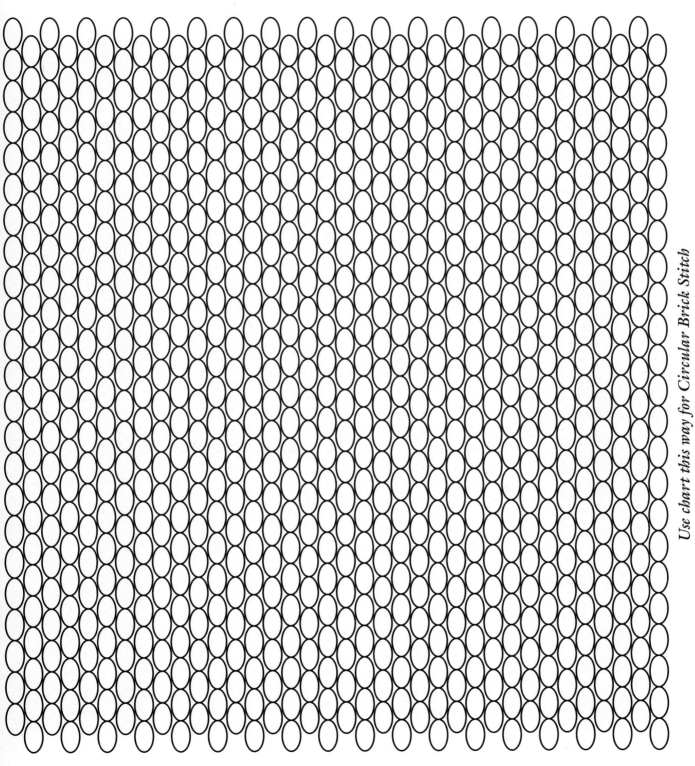

Use chart this way for Peyote Stitch

Use chart this way for Circular Brick Stitch